PASTRY
CLASSICS

Consultant Editor:
Valerie Ferguson

HERMES
HOUSE

Contents

Introduction

What could be nicer than a fruit pie, all golden crust and juicy fruit, or perhaps a delicious seafood tart, crispy vegetarian strudel or steak and kidney pie, rich and mellow on a chilly winter's day? The list is as long as you choose to make it. Dreaming about one pastry classic triggers thoughts of another, and all are bound up with other memories: grandmothers with floury elbows rolling out pastry with the ease of long practice; children shaping grubby bits of dough into their initials; hot pies cooling on windowsills.

Times may have changed but pastry is as popular as ever. Even busy people can make pastry: there is always the option of making up batches of rubbed-in mixture at moments of leisure and freezing them for later use. Every supermarket stocks frozen pastry, which is a boon to the busy cook. Few of us choose to make our own puff pastry, except for special occasions, but before you reach for the packet of frozen shortcrust, consider how simple that pastry is to make.

The mouth-watering collection of recipes in this book includes pastry classics for all courses and every occasion. So get out that rolling pin and give the family a treat.

Types of Pastry

Shortcrust Pastry

One of the easiest and most versatile of pastries, shortcrust consists of flour and fat, with just enough liquid to bind the ingredients together. Always use iced water and, if time permits, wrap shortcrust pastry in clear film and chill it for 30 minutes before rolling it out.

Rich Shortcrust Pastry

Richer than plain shortcrust, this sets to a crisper crust. It is often used for fruit pies. Use the standard shortcrust recipe but always use butter and substitute an egg yolk for part of the liquid. For a sweet pastry, add 10–15 ml/ 2–3 tsp caster sugar after rubbing in the fat.

Puff Pastry

This is made in such a way that it separates into crisp, melt-in-the-mouth layers when cooked, thanks to the air trapped in it. A block of butter is wrapped in a basic dough; the pastry is then turned, rolled, folded and chilled several times. If using frozen puff pastry, thaw slowly.

Rough Puff Pastry

Diced fat is mixed with the flour but not rubbed in, so that when the liquid is added, a dough is formed in which the fat can be seen. The pastry is rolled and folded several times before being rested and baked. The fat for rough puff pastry should be very cold and it is helpful if the flour is chilled before use.

Choux Pastry

To make choux pastry, the butter is melted with water and then the flour is added all at once and vigorously beaten in before the eggs are added. The uncooked mixture is more of a paste than a pastry. It is easy to make, but the ingredients must be carefully measured.

Filo Pastry

This traditional Greek pastry comes ready-rolled in paper-thin sheets, which are layered, then cooked until crisp. It is made with very little fat so each layer must be brushed with oil or melted butter. It dries out quickly when exposed to the air so any pastry not in use should be kept covered with a clean, damp dish towel.

Flaky Pastry

This involves making a dough with half the stipulated amount of butter, then softening the rest to the same consistency as the dough and dotting it over the surface of the rolled-out pastry. The pastry is then folded, turned, rolled and chilled several times. When it is baked, it separates into crisp leaves that are beautifully light.

Hot Water Crust Pastry

Hot liquid is added to the dry ingredients and the pastry is kept warm while resting to prevent it breaking up when rolled out. It is traditionally used for raised pies.

Techniques

Rubbing in

Add the diced fat to the flour. Using the fingertips and thumbs, draw up a small amount of mixture and rub together to break it down into crumbs. Repeat the process, lifting the mixture each time to incorporate air, until no large lumps of fat remain. Do not overwork the dough.

Glazing

For a rich, golden crust, brush the pastry with beaten egg, a mixture of beaten egg and water, or milk before baking. For a sweet pie, you can add a light dusting of caster sugar.

Crimping a Pastry Shell

Make a 'V' with the forefinger and second finger of your right hand, pressing down lightly on the pastry. Then use the index finger of your left hand to push the pastry between the 'V' inwards. Or press the knuckle of one hand against the inner edge, using the other hand to pinch the dough around your finger into a 'V'.

Baking Blind

This refers to the method of partially or fully baking an unfilled pastry case. Line it with non-stick baking paper and add an even layer of baking beans (use dried beans kept for the purpose or special china beans). Bake for 10 minutes, then remove the paper and beans and return the pastry case to the oven for 5 minutes more, or longer if it is not to be cooked again.

Using a Pastry Blender

A pastry blender is a gadget comprising 5–8 arched wires on a wooden handle. Some cooks prefer it for rubbing in as it stops warm hands softening the fat, but it can break down the fat almost too efficiently. Use the blender for half the fat, and add the rest in pea-size pieces.

Rolling Out & Lining a Tin

A neat pastry case that doesn't distort or shrink in baking is the desired result. The key to success is handling the dough gently.

1 Using even pressure, roll out the dough, from the centre to the edge.

2 Give the dough a quarter turn from time to time during the rolling. Continue rolling out until the dough circle is about 5 cm/2 in larger than the tin. It will be about 3 mm/⅛ in thick.

3 Set the rolling pin on the dough, near one side. Fold the outside edge of dough over the pin, then roll the pin to wrap the dough around it. Hold the pin over the tin and gently unroll the dough so it drapes into the tin.

4 With your fingertips, lift and ease the dough into the tin, gently pressing it over the base and up the side. Turn excess dough over the rim and trim it with a knife or scissors.

Making Pastry in a Food Processor

Process the flour, salt and fat, turning the machine on and off, just until the mixture is crumbly. Add the iced water and process again just until the dough starts to pull away from the sides of the bowl. Remove from the processor, gather into a ball, wrap and chill.

Making Shortcrust Pastry

The pastry dough can be made with half butter or margarine and half white vegetable fat, or with all one kind of fat.

Makes 350 g/12 oz pastry, enough to line a 23 cm/9 in pastry case

INGREDIENTS
225 g/8 oz/2 cups plain white flour
1.5 ml/¼ tsp salt
115 g/4 oz/½ cup fat, chilled and diced
45–60 ml/3–4 tbsp iced water

1 Sift the flour and salt into a bowl. Add the fat. Rub it into the flour with your fingertips until the mixture resembles breadcrumbs.

2 Sprinkle 45 ml/3 tbsp water over the mixture. With a fork, toss gently to mix and moisten it.

3 Press the dough into a ball. If it is too dry to form a dough, add the remaining water.

4 Wrap the ball of dough in clear film and chill in the fridge for 30 minutes before using.

Leek & Broccoli Tartlets

These melt-in-the-mouth tartlet cases are made from a rich, buttery pastry, flavoured with grated cheese.

Serves 4

INGREDIENTS
175 g/6 oz/1½ cups plain flour, sifted
115 g/4 oz/½ cup butter, diced
25 g/1 oz finely grated Pecorino cheese
    or young, mild Parmesan
60–90 ml/4–6 tbsp water
2 small leeks, sliced
75 g/3 oz tiny broccoli florets
150 ml/¼ pint/⅔ cup milk
2 eggs
few pinches ground mace
30 ml/2 tbsp double cream
salt and freshly ground black pepper
15 g/½ oz/2 tbsp flaked almonds, toasted,
    and a sprig of fresh sage, to garnish

2 Preheat the oven to 190°C/375°F/ Gas 5. Roll out the pastry on a floured surface and use to line four 10 cm/ 4 in tartlet tins. Line the pastry cases and bake blind for 15 minutes, then remove the paper and cook for a further 5 minutes.

3 To make the filling, place the vegetables in a pan and cook them in the milk for 2–3 minutes. Strain the milk into a small bowl and whisk in the eggs, mace, cream and seasoning.

VARIATION: You could also try different vegetables such as sliced courgettes and sliced red pepper or broad beans and mushroom depending on the season or what you have available.

1 Blend the flour, butter and grated cheese together in a food processor to give a fine crumb consistency. Add salt to taste. Stir in enough water to bring the pastry together in a ball. Chill for 15 minutes.

4 Arrange the vegetables in the pastry cases and pour over the egg mixture. Bake for 20 minutes, or until the filling is just firm. Leave to cool slightly, then carefully remove the tarts from the tins. Sprinkle with almonds before serving warm or cold, garnished with a sprig of sage.

Red Pepper & Watercress Filo Parcels

Filo pastry has a unique crisp texture and an attractive appearance so these parcels would be a good choice for a dinner party.

Makes 8

INGREDIENTS
3 red peppers
175 g/6 oz watercress
225 g/8 oz/1 cup Ricotta cheese
50 g/2 oz/½ cup blanched almonds, toasted
  and chopped
salt and freshly ground black pepper
8 sheets of filo pastry, thawed if frozen
30 ml/2 tbsp olive oil
salad leaves, to serve

3 Add the Ricotta and almonds, mix well and season to taste.

1 Preheat the oven to 190°C/375°F/ Gas 5. Place the peppers under a hot grill until blistered and charred. Place in a plastic bag. When cool enough to handle, peel, seed and pat dry on kitchen paper.

2 Place the peppers and watercress in a food processor and pulse until coarsely chopped. Spoon into a bowl.

4 Working with one sheet of filo pastry at a time, cut out two 18 cm/ 7 in and two 5 cm/2 in squares from each sheet. Brush one large square with a little olive oil and place a second large square at an angle of 90 degrees to form a star shape.

5 Place a small square in the centre of the star shape, brush lightly with oil and top with a second small square.

6 Top with one-eighth of the red pepper mixture. Bring the edges together to form a purse shape and twist to seal. Place on a lightly greased baking sheet and cook for 25–30 minutes, until golden. Serve hot, accompanied by crisp salad leaves.

Prawn Rolls

Here, versatile filo pastry is used for delightful little prawn-filled rolls, fried in minutes to crisp perfection.

Makes about 24

INGREDIENTS
15 ml/1 tbsp olive oil
15 g/½ oz/1 tbsp butter, for the filling
2–3 spring onions, finely chopped
15 g/½ oz/2 tbsp plain flour
300 ml/½ pint/1¼ cups milk
2.5 ml/½ tsp paprika
350 g/12 oz cooked peeled prawns, deveined
40 g/1½ oz/3 tbsp butter, melted
8 sheets filo pastry, thawed if frozen
sunflower oil, for frying
salt and freshly ground white pepper
spring onion and coriander leaves,
    to garnish
ground cinnamon and icing sugar,
    to serve (optional)

1 First make the filling. Heat the butter and olive oil in a saucepan and fry the spring onions over a very low heat for 2–3 minutes, until soft. Stir in the flour, and then gradually add the milk to make a smooth sauce.

2 Season the sauce with paprika, salt and pepper. Chop the prawns and stir them into the sauce.

3 Take a sheet of filo pastry and cut it in half widthways, to make a rectangle about 18 x 14 cm/7 x 5½ in. Cover the remaining pastry with clear film to prevent it from drying out.

4 Brush one rectangle of filo pastry with melted butter and then place a heaped teaspoon of filling at one end. Roll up like a cigar, tucking in the sides as you go. Continue in this way until you have used all the filling.

5 Heat about 1 cm/½ in sunflower oil in a heavy-based pan and fry the rolls, in batches, for 2–3 minutes until golden, turning occasionally.

6 Drain on kitchen paper and then serve garnished with a spring onion and coriander leaves, and sprinkled with cinnamon and icing sugar, if liked.

Spinach Turnovers

Light-as-air puff pastry encloses a surprising and delicious filling.

Makes 20

INGREDIENTS
25 g/1 oz/2 tbsp raisins, soaked in warm
    water for 10 minutes and drained
25 ml/1½ tbsp olive oil
450 g/1 lb fresh spinach, chopped
6 drained canned anchovies, chopped
2 garlic cloves, finely chopped
25 g/1 oz/⅓ cup pine nuts, chopped
butter, for greasing
350 g/12 oz puff pastry, thawed if frozen
1 egg, beaten
salt and freshly ground black pepper

1 Roughly chop the raisins. Heat the
oil in a frying pan, stir in the spinach,
cover and cook over a low heat for
about 2 minutes. Uncover, increase the
heat and let any liquid evaporate.

2 Add the anchovies, garlic and
seasoning. Cook, stirring, for 1 minute.
Remove from the heat, add the raisins
and pine nuts, and cool.

3 Preheat the oven to 180°C/350°F/
Gas 4. Lightly grease a baking sheet.
Roll out the puff pastry to a 3 mm/
⅛ in thickness. Using a 7.5 cm/3 in
pastry cutter, cut out 20 rounds.

4 Place two teaspoons of the filling in
the middle of each round, brush the
edges with water, bring up the sides
of the pastry and seal. Press the edges
together with the back of a fork.
Brush with egg. Place the turnovers
on the baking sheet and bake for
about 15 minutes, until golden.
Serve warm.

Cheese Aigrettes

These choux pastry buns can be prepared ahead, then deep fried to serve.

Makes 30

INGREDIENTS
100 g/3¾ oz/scant 1 cup strong plain flour
2.5 ml/½ tsp paprika
2.5 ml/½ tsp salt
75 g/3 oz/6 tbsp cold butter, diced
200 ml/7 fl oz/scant 1 cup water
3 eggs, beaten
75 g/3 oz/¾ cup coarsely grated mature
    Gruyère cheese
corn or vegetable oil, for deep frying
50 g/2 oz/⅔ cup freshly grated
    Parmesan cheese
freshly ground black pepper
flat leaf parsley sprigs, to garnish

1 Sift the flour, paprika and salt on to a sheet of greaseproof paper. Add black pepper to taste.

2 Heat the butter and water in a saucepan. As soon as the butter has melted and the liquid starts to boil, tip in all the flour and beat with a wooden spoon until the paste comes away from the sides of the pan.

3 Remove the pan from the heat and cool for 5 minutes. Gradually beat in enough of the egg to give a stiff dropping consistency that still holds its shape on the spoon. Mix in the cheese.

4 Heat the oil to 180°C/350°F. Deep fry teaspoonfuls of the choux pastry in batches for 3–4 minutes, until golden brown. Drain on kitchen paper. Pile the aigrettes on a warmed serving dish, sprinkle with Parmesan and garnish with parsley.

Spicy Meat-filled Parcels

These appetizing little filo parcels can be shallow fried or baked in the oven – they are equally delicious whichever way they are cooked.

Makes 16

INGREDIENTS
450 g/1 lb/4 cups lean minced beef
2 small onions, finely chopped
2 small leeks, very finely chopped
2 garlic cloves, crushed
10 ml/2 tsp coriander seeds, dry fried
    and ground
5 ml/1 tsp cumin seeds, dry fried and ground
5–10 ml/1–2 tsp mild curry powder
2 eggs, beaten
16 sheets filo pastry, thawed if frozen
45–60 ml/3–4 tbsp sunflower oil
milk, for brushing, if needed
salt and freshly ground black pepper
sunflower oil, for frying
light soy sauce, to serve

1 To make the filling, mix the meat with the onions, leeks, garlic, coriander, cumin, curry powder and seasoning. Cook in a heated wok, without oil, stirring constantly, for 5 minutes, until the meat has changed colour and looks cooked.

2 Cool, then mix in enough beaten egg to bind the mixture to a soft consistency. Any leftover egg can be used to seal the edges of the dough; otherwise, use milk.

3 Brush a sheet of filo with oil, lay another sheet on top and cut in half. Place a tablespoonful of the filling on each double piece of filo. Fold the sides to the middle so that the edges just overlap and brush with beaten egg or milk. Fold the other two sides to the middle to make a square parcel. Make 15 more parcels and place on a floured tray in the fridge.

VARIATION: If preferred, these parcels can be made using spring roll wrappers available from Chinese supermarkets.

4 Heat about 1 cm/½ in sunflower oil in a shallow pan and cook the parcels, in batches, for 3 minutes on the first side, then turn them over and cook for a further 2 minutes, or until they are thoroughly heated through. Serve hot, sprinkled with light soy sauce.

5 If preferred, these spicy parcels can be cooked in a hot oven at 200°C/ 400°F/Gas 6 for 20 minutes. Glaze with more beaten egg before baking for a rich, golden colour.

Wrapped Salmon & Rice

This dish is made with chunks of fresh salmon, combined with mushrooms, eggs and rice in light and flaky pastry.

Serves 4

INGREDIENTS

450 g/1 lb skinned and boned fresh
    salmon fillet
115 g/4 oz/1½ cups button mushrooms
50 g/2 oz/4 tbsp butter
6 spring onions, finely sliced
2 eggs, hard-boiled
175 g/6 oz/1 cup long grain rice, cooked
juice of ½ lemon
450 g/1 lb puff pastry, thawed if frozen
1 egg, beaten
salt and freshly ground black pepper

1 Put the salmon fillet into a saucepan with just enough water to cover it. Poach it gently for 10 minutes, until just cooked. Drain and then leave to cool.

2 Roughly chop the mushrooms. Melt the butter in a saucepan and cook the mushrooms and spring onions for 2–3 minutes until just softened. Place them in a mixing bowl.

3 Flake the fish and add to the mushroom and onion mixture. Chop the eggs and stir into the salmon mixture with the rice. Stir in the lemon juice and season well with salt and pepper. Preheat the oven to 200°C/400°F/Gas 6.

4 Roll out the puff pastry to a rectangle 30 x 35 cm/12 x 14 in. Brush the edges with egg. Spoon the filling into the centre of the pastry. Bring the sides of the pastry to the centre and seal together. Fold over the ends, seal with egg, then turn the pie over.

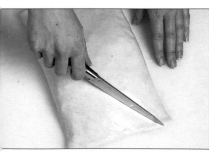

5 Score the top of the pastry with a knife and brush with the remaining egg. Place on a baking sheet and bake for about 30 minutes, until golden. Serve hot, or leave to cool completely and serve cold.

Golden Fish Pie

Crumpled sheets of filo pastry make a decorative topping and their crispness contrasts delightfully with the creamy fish pie.

Serves 4–6

INGREDIENTS

675 g/1½ lb white fish fillets
300 ml/½ pint/1¼ cups milk
flavouring ingredients (onion slices, bay leaf and black peppercorns)
115 g/4 oz cooked, peeled prawns, deveined
115 g/4 oz/½ cup butter
50 g/2 oz/½ cup plain flour
300 ml/½ pint/1¼ cups single cream
75 g/3 oz/¾ cup grated Gruyère cheese
1 bunch watercress, leaves only, chopped
5 ml/1 tsp Dijon mustard
5 sheets filo pastry, thawed if frozen
salt and freshly ground black pepper

2 Strain the fish and reserve the milk. Skin and bone the fish, then roughly flake into a shallow ovenproof dish. Scatter the prawns over the fish.

3 Melt 50 g/2 oz/4 tbsp of the butter in a pan. Stir in the flour and cook for 1 minute. Stir in the reserved milk and the cream. Bring to the boil, stirring, then simmer for 2–3 minutes, until the sauce has thickened.

1 Place the fish fillets in a pan, pour over the milk and add the flavouring ingredients. Bring just to the boil, then cover and simmer for 10–12 minutes, until the fish is almost tender.

4 Remove the pan from the heat and stir in the Gruyère, watercress, mustard and seasoning to taste. Pour over the fish and leave to cool.

5 Preheat the oven to 190°C/375°F/Gas 5. Melt the remaining butter. Brush one sheet of filo pastry with a little butter, then crumple up loosely and place on top of the filling. Repeat with the remaining filo sheets and butter until they are all used up and the pie is completely covered.

6 Bake in the oven for 25–30 minutes, until the pastry is golden and crisp and the pie is heated through.

VARIATION: Two hard-boiled eggs, chopped, can be substituted for the prawns.

Herbed Halibut Millefeuilles

The crisp puff pastry balances the creamy fish and the herbs add their own special flavours.

Serves 4

INGREDIENTS
250 g/9 oz puff pastry, thawed if frozen
butter, for greasing
1 egg, beaten
1 small onion, chopped
5 ml/1 tsp grated fresh
    root ginger
7.5 ml/1½ tsp oil
150 ml/¼ pint/⅔ cup fish stock
15 ml/1 tbsp dry sherry
350 g/12 oz halibut, cooked
    and flaked
225 g/8 oz white crab meat
1 avocado
juice of 1 lime
1 mango
salt and freshly ground
    black pepper
15 ml/1 tbsp chopped mixed parsley,
    thyme and chives, to garnish

3 Let the pastry cool on a wire rack for a few minutes, then cut it across twice in one direction and once in the other to make six pieces. Leave to cool completely.

4 Fry the onion and ginger in the oil until tender. Add the stock and sherry and simmer for 5 minutes. Add the halibut and crab meat and season to taste. Peel and chop the avocado and toss in the lime juice. Peel and chop the mango, reserving a few slices for garnishing. Add both to the fish.

VARIATION: You could substitute salmon and cooked, peeled prawns for the halibut and crab meat, if you prefer.

1 Roll the pastry out into a square 25 x 25 cm/10 x 10 in, trim the edges and place on a greased baking sheet. Prick all over with a fork, then rest the pastry in the fridge for 30 minutes.

2 Preheat the oven to 230°C/450°F/ Gas 8. Brush the top of the pastry with beaten egg, and bake for 10–15 minutes, or until golden brown.

5 Using three layers of pastry for each millefeuille, build up alternate layers of fish and pastry, starting and finishing with pastry. Carefully cut each stack in half. Serve garnished with herbs and mango slices.

Trout with Filo Crust

Wrapped in pastry and filled with an almond stuffing, this trout is transformed into a special dish for a dinner party.

Serves 4

INGREDIENTS
75 g/3 oz/6 tbsp butter
1 small onion, finely chopped
115 g/4 oz/1 cup ground almonds
30 ml/2 tbsp chopped fresh parsley
finely grated rind of 1 lemon
4 x 175 g/6 oz trout, gutted
12 sheets filo pastry, thawed if frozen
salt and freshly ground black pepper
lemon slices and parsley, to garnish

1 Preheat the oven to 200°C/400°F/ Gas 6. Melt 25 g/1 oz/2 tbsp of the butter in a saucepan and cook the onion until soft, but not coloured.

2 Add 75 g/3 oz/¾ cup of the ground almonds with the parsley and lemon. Season the trout and stuff the inside cavities of the fish.

3 Melt the remaining butter. Cut the filo pastry into strips and brush with the butter. Wrap the strips around the fish to enclose it completely. Place on a greased baking sheet.

4 Sprinkle the remaining ground almonds over the pastry and bake for 20–25 minutes, until golden brown. Serve the trout garnished with thin lemon slices and a sprig of fresh parsley.

Crab & Prawn Filo Tart

With its delicately frilled filo crust, this elegant seafood and curd cheese tart looks almost too good to eat.

Serves 4–6

INGREDIENTS

2 eggs, beaten
150 ml/¼ pint/⅔ cup milk
30 ml/2 tbsp pastis (optional)
200 g/7 oz crab meat
200 g/7 oz cooked peeled
　prawns, deveined
225 g/8 oz/1 cup curd cheese
115 g/4 oz/1½ cups
　mushrooms, chopped
10 sheets filo pastry, thawed if frozen
50 g/2 oz/¼ cup butter, melted
salt and freshly ground
　black pepper
50 g/2 oz/⅔ cup Parmesan cheese
　shavings, to garnish

1 Preheat the oven to 190°C/375°F/ Gas 5. Grease a deep 18 cm/7 in flan tin. Mix together the eggs, milk, pastis, if using, crab meat, prawns, curd cheese and mushrooms in a bowl. Season to taste with salt and pepper.

2 Line the flan tin with filo pastry, placing the sheets at alternate angles and brushing each one with a little of the melted butter. Leave the excess pastry hanging over the sides of the tin.

3 Spoon in the filling. Fold the excess pastry over, crumpling it to make a decorative edge. Brush with melted butter and bake for 35–40 minutes. Scatter the Parmesan over before serving.

Deep-sea Scallops with Wild Mushrooms

Puff pastry is shaped into edible "shells" for a novel way of serving seafood.

Serves 4

INGREDIENTS
350 g/12 oz puff pastry, thawed if frozen
1 egg, beaten, to glaze
75 g/3 oz/6 tbsp unsalted butter
12 scallops, trimmed and
   thickly sliced
2 shallots, chopped
½ stick celery, cut into strips
½ medium carrot, cut into strips
225 g/8 oz/3 cups mixed wild
   mushrooms, sliced
60 ml/4 tbsp dry vermouth
150 ml/¼ pint/⅔ cup crème fraîche
4 egg yolks
celery salt and cayenne pepper
15 ml/1 tbsp lemon juice
salt and freshly ground black pepper
salad leaves, to serve

1 Roll the pastry out on a floured surface, cut into four 13 cm/5 in rounds, then trim into shell shapes. Brush with a little beaten egg and mark a shell pattern on each with a small knife. Place on a baking sheet and rest in the fridge for 30 minutes. Preheat the oven to 200°C/400°F/Gas 6.

2 Melt 25 g/1 oz/2 tbsp of the butter in a pan, season the scallops and cook over a high heat for no longer than 30 seconds. Transfer to a plate.

3 Bake the pastry shapes for 20–25 minutes, until golden. Fry the shallots, celery and carrot gently in the remaining butter without colouring. Add the mushrooms and cook over a moderate heat until the juices begin to run. Pour in the vermouth and increase the heat to evaporate the juices.

4 Add the crème fraîche and scallops and bring to a simmer (do not boil). Remove the pan from the heat and blend in the egg yolks. Return the pan to a low heat and cook for a minute until the sauce has thickened to the consistency of thin cream.

5 Remove the pan from the heat. Season with celery salt and cayenne pepper and add the lemon juice.

6 Split the pastry shapes open and place the bases on four plates. Spoon the filling over the pastry bases and replace the tops. Serve immediately with crisp salad leaves.

Old-fashioned Chicken Pie

This traditional single-crust pie would make a filling family supper for a chilly winter evening.

Serves 4

INGREDIENTS
1.5 kg/3–3½ lb chicken
1 onion, quartered
1 fresh tarragon or rosemary sprig
300 ml/½ pint/1¼ cups water
25 g/1 oz/2 tbsp butter
115 g/4 oz/1½ cups button mushrooms
30 ml/2 tbsp plain flour
300 ml/½ pint/1¼ cups
   chicken stock
115 g/4 oz/¾ cup cooked ham, diced
30 ml/2 tbsp chopped
   fresh parsley
450 g/1 lb puff or flaky pastry, thawed
   if frozen
1 egg, beaten
salt and freshly ground black pepper

1 Preheat the oven to 200°C/400°F/ Gas 6. Put the chicken into a casserole together with the quartered onion, the herb and water, and season with salt and pepper. Cover and cook for about 1¼ hours, or until tender.

2 Remove the chicken and strain the liquid into a measuring jug or bowl. Cool and remove any fat that settles on the surface. Make up to 300 ml/ ½ pint/1¼ cups with water and reserve for the sauce.

3 Remove the chicken from the bones and cut into large cubes. Melt the butter in a pan, add the mushrooms and cook for 2–3 minutes. Sprinkle in the flour and gradually blend in the chicken stock.

4 Bring to the boil, season and add the ham, chicken and parsley. Turn into one large, or four small, pie dishes. Cool before covering with pastry.

5 Preheat the oven to 200°C/400°F/ Gas 6. Roll out the pastry on a lightly floured surface to 5 cm/2 in larger than the pie dish. Cut a narrow strip of pastry. Dampen with a little water, stick to the rim of the dish and brush the strip with beaten egg.

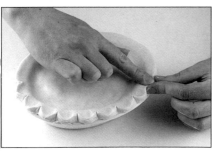

6 Lay the pastry loosely over the filling, taking care not to stretch it. Press firmly on to the rim. Trim away the excess pastry and knock up the sides using a knife. Crimp the edge neatly and cut a hole in the centre of the pie. Decorate with pastry leaves, glaze with beaten egg and bake for 30 minutes, until golden.

Chicken, Cheese & Leek Jalousie

A jalousie is a family-size lattice pastry roll with a mild, creamy filling. This would be a good choice for informal entertaining.

Serves 6

INGREDIENTS
1.5 kg/3–3½ lb roasted chicken
2 large leeks, thinly sliced
2 garlic cloves, crushed
40 g/1½ oz/3 tbsp butter
115 g/4 oz/1¾ cups button
   mushrooms, sliced
200 g/7 oz/scant 1 cup cream cheese
grated rind of 1 small lemon
45 ml/3 tbsp chopped fresh parsley
500 g/1¼ lb puff pastry, thawed if frozen
1 egg, beaten
salt and freshly ground black pepper
fresh herbs, to garnish

1 Strip the meat from the chicken, discarding the skin and bones. Chop or shred the meat and set it aside.

2 Sauté the leeks and garlic in the butter for 10 minutes. Stir in the mushrooms and cook for 5 minutes. Leave to cool, then add the cream cheese, lemon rind, parsley and salt and pepper. Cool completely, then stir in the chicken.

COOK'S TIP: The chicken could be cooked the day before the jalousie is prepared.

3 Roll out the pastry on a lightly floured work surface to a rectangle about 35 x 25 cm/14 x 10 in. Transfer to a non-stick baking sheet. Spoon the filling on to the pastry, leaving a generous margin at top and bottom, and 10 cm/4 in on each side. Cut the pastry sides diagonally up to the filling at 2 cm/¾ in intervals.

4 Brush the edges of the pastry with the beaten egg. Draw the strips over each other in alternate crosses to "plait". Seal the top and bottom edges. Glaze with beaten egg. Allow it to rest.

5 Preheat the oven to 200°C/400°F/ Gas 6. Bake for 15 minutes, then lower the oven temperature to 190°C/375°F/ Gas 5 and bake for 15 minutes, or until the pastry is golden and crisp. Leave for 10 minutes before sliding the jalousie on to a board or platter to serve. Garnish with fresh herbs.

Turkey & Cranberry Pie

This is a traditional raised pie made with hot water crust pastry, which can be tricky to handle, but is worth the effort.

Serves 8

INGREDIENTS
450 g/1 lb/4 cups pork sausagemeat
450 g/1 lb/4 cups minced pork
15 ml/1 tbsp ground coriander
15 ml/1 tbsp dried mixed herbs
finely grated rind of 2
   large oranges
10 ml/2 tsp grated fresh root ginger or
   2.5 ml/½ tsp ground ginger
10 ml/2 tsp salt
freshly ground black pepper
450 g/1 lb/4 cups plain flour
5 ml/1 tsp salt
150 g/5 oz/⅔ cup lard
150 ml/¼ pint/⅔ cup mixed milk
   and water
450 g/1 lb turkey breast fillets,
   thinly sliced
115 g/4 oz/1 cup fresh cranberries
1 egg, beaten
300 ml/½ pint/1¼ cups aspic jelly,
   made up as packet instructions

1 Preheat the oven to 180°C/350°F/ Gas 4. Place a baking tray in the oven to preheat. In a bowl, mix together the sausagemeat, pork, coriander, herbs, orange rind, ginger and salt and pepper. Set aside.

2 To make the pastry, put the flour into a large bowl with the salt. Heat the lard in a small pan with the milk and water until just beginning to boil. Draw the pan aside and allow to cool slightly. Using a wooden spoon, quickly stir the liquid into the flour until a very stiff dough is formed. Turn on to a work surface and knead the dough until smooth.

3 Cut one-third off the dough for the lid, wrap it in clear film and keep it in a warm place. Roll out the large piece of dough on a floured surface and line the base and sides of a well-greased 20 cm/8 in loose-based, springform cake tin. Work with the dough while it is still warm, as it will crack and break if it is allowed to get cold. Preheat the oven to 200°C/400°F/Gas 6.

COOK'S TIP: Cranberry sauce can be used if fresh cranberries are not available.

4 Put the turkey breast fillets between two pieces of clear film and flatten with a rolling pin. Spoon half the pork mixture into the base of the tin, pressing it well into the edges. Cover with half the turkey slices and then the cranberries, followed by the remaining turkey and finally the rest of the pork mixture.

5 Roll out the remaining dough and cover the filling, trimming any excess and sealing the edges with beaten egg. Make a steam hole in the centre and decorate the top. Brush with beaten egg and bake for 2 hours. Transfer to a wire rack to cool. When cold, use a funnel to fill the pipe with liquid aspic jelly. Leave to set overnight.

Boeuf en Croûte

Individual crisp, golden puff pastry parcels are filled with fillet steak topped with a mouth-watering mushroom filling.

Serves 4

INGREDIENTS
Dijon mustard
4 fillet steaks, about
    115–150 g/4–5 oz each
freshly ground black pepper
25 g/1 oz/2 tbsp butter
25 g/1 oz/2 tbsp butter, for the filling
4 shallots, finely chopped
1–2 garlic cloves, crushed
225–275 g/8–10 oz/3–3¾ cups flat
    mushrooms, finely chopped
15 ml/1 tbsp finely chopped
    fresh parsley
salt and freshly ground black pepper
275 g/10 oz puff pastry, thawed
    if frozen
25 g/1 oz/½ cup fresh white breadcrumbs
beaten egg, for glazing
parsley or chervil sprigs,
    to garnish
French beans and boiled new potatoes,
    to serve

1 Preheat the oven to 220°C/425°F/ Gas 7. Rub a little mustard over each of the steaks and season with pepper. Melt the butter in a heavy-based frying pan and fry the steaks for about 1–2 minutes each side, so that they are browned on the outside but still red in the centre. Transfer to a plate to cool.

2 To make the filling, melt the butter and fry the shallots and garlic briefly. Stir in the finely chopped mushrooms. Fry over a fairly high heat for about 3–4 minutes, stirring, until the juices run. Lower the heat and cook gently for 4–5 minutes until the mixture is dry. Add the parsley and seasoning and leave to cool.

3 Cut the pastry into four and roll out each piece very thinly to a 18 cm/7 in square. Cut the corners from each square and spread a spoonful of the mushroom mixture in the centre. Top with a steak and sprinkle with a spoonful of fresh breadcrumbs.

4 Bring the sides of the pastry up to the centre and seal with water. Place seam-side down on a baking sheet. Decorate with pastry trimmings and brush with beaten egg. Bake for about 20 minutes, until golden brown. Garnish with parsley or chervil and serve with French beans and boiled new potatoes.

Beef Pasties

Easily made with shortcrust pastry, these popular pasties are filling, nourishing and, above all, scrumptious.

Serves 8

INGREDIENTS
350 g/12 oz/3 cups plain white flour
2.5 ml/½ tsp salt
175 g/6 oz/⅔ cup fat, chilled and diced
60–75 ml/5–6 tbsp iced water
15 ml/1 tbsp oil
175 g/6 oz/1½ cups minced beef
15 ml/1 tbsp tomato purée
1 onion, chopped
1 carrot, diced
50 g/2 oz turnip, diced
1 large potato, diced
25 g/1 oz/¼ cup plain flour
150 ml/¼ pint/⅔ cup beef stock
15 ml/1 tbsp chopped fresh parsley
1 egg, beaten
salt and freshly ground black pepper
salad, to serve

1 Make the shortcrust pastry following the instructions from the techniques section. Wrap in clear film and rest in the fridge for 30 minutes. Preheat the oven to 190°C/375°F/Gas 5. Heat the oil in a large pan and add the minced beef. Cook for 5 minutes. Stir in the tomato purée, onion, carrot, turnip and potato. Cook for a further 5 minutes.

2 Add the flour and cook for 1 minute. Stir in the stock and season with salt and pepper to taste. Cook over a low heat for 10 minutes. Stir in the fresh parsley and cool.

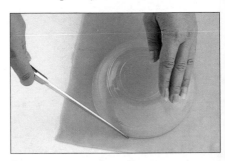

3 Roll out the pastry to a large rectangle. Cut eight 15 cm/6 in rounds using a suitable small bowl or saucer as a guide.

COOK'S TIP: Do not overfill the pasties or the filling will burst through the pastry during cooking.

4 Spoon the filling on to one half of each pastry round, brush the edges with egg and fold in half. Crimp the edges to seal. Brush the pasties with egg and place on a baking sheet. Cook for 35 minutes, or until golden. Serve with a crisp salad.

Steak & Kidney Pie

This traditional double-crust pie is a warming and tasty treat on cold winter evenings.

Serves 4

INGREDIENTS
450 g/1 lb puff pastry, thawed if frozen
45 ml/3 tbsp flour
675 g/1½ lb rump steak, cubed
175 g/6 oz pig's or
  lamb's kidney
25 g/1 oz/2 tbsp butter
1 onion, chopped
15 ml/1 tbsp English mustard
2 bay leaves
15 ml/1 tbsp chopped
  fresh parsley
150 ml/¼ pint/⅔ cup beef stock
1 egg, beaten
salt and freshly ground
  black pepper

2 Put the flour, seasoned with salt and pepper, in a bowl and toss the cubes of steak in it. Remove all fat and skin from the kidneys and slice them thickly. Add to the bowl with the steak cubes and toss well. Melt the butter in a pan and fry the onion until soft, then stir in the mustard, bay leaves, parsley and stock.

3 Preheat the oven to 190°C/375°F/ Gas 5. Place the steak and kidney in the pie and pour over the onion and stock mixture.

1 Roll out two-thirds of the pastry on a lightly floured surface to a thickness of 3 mm/⅛ in and line a 1.5 litre/2½ pint/6¼ cup pie dish. Place a pie funnel in the middle.

4 Roll out the remaining pastry to a thickness of 3 mm/⅛ in to make the lid. Brush the edges of the pastry in the dish with beaten egg and cover with the pastry lid. Press the two layers of pastry together to seal the edge, then trim. Knock up the edge using a knife. Use the trimmings to decorate the top in a leaf pattern.

5 Brush the pie with beaten egg and make a small hole over the top of the funnel. Bake for about 1 hour, until the pastry is golden brown.

VARIATION: If preferred, the kidneys could be replaced with button mushrooms. Shortcrust pastry also works well in place of puff.

Wild Mushroom Pie

Home-made flaky pastry makes this wonderful pie ideal for a special occasion. Serve it garnished with light pastry shapes.

Serves 6

INGREDIENTS
225 g/8 oz/2 cups plain flour
2.5 ml/½ tsp salt
50 g/2 oz/4 tbsp solid vegetable fat
10 ml/2 tsp lemon juice
about 150 ml/¼ pint/⅔ cup water
115 g/4 oz/½ cup butter, chilled
    and cubed, for pastry
150 g/5 oz/⅔ cup butter
2 shallots, finely chopped
2 garlic cloves, crushed
450 g/1 lb/6½ cups mixed wild
    mushrooms, sliced
45 ml/3 tbsp chopped fresh parsley
30 ml/2 tbsp double cream
1 egg, beaten, to glaze
salt and freshly ground black pepper

1 To make the pastry, sift the flour and salt together into a large bowl. Add the fat and rub into the mixture until it resembles breadcrumbs.

2 Add the lemon juice and enough iced water to make a soft, but not sticky dough. Cover and rest in the fridge for 20 minutes.

3 Roll out the pastry into a rectangle on a lightly floured surface. Mark the dough into three equal strips and arrange half the butter cubes over two-thirds of the dough.

4 Fold the covered two-thirds over, folding the uncovered third last. Seal the edges. Give the dough a quarter turn and roll it out again. Mark it into thirds and dot with the remaining butter cubes, fold and roll. Chill the pastry for 20 minutes. Fold, roll and chill the pastry 3 more times.

5 For the filling, melt 50 g/2 oz/ 4 tbsp butter and fry the shallots and garlic until soft. Add the remaining butter and the mushrooms and cook for 35–40 minutes. Drain off any liquid and add the remaining ingredients. Cool. Preheat the oven to 220°C/425°F/Gas 7.

6 Divide the pastry in two. Roll out one piece into a 23 cm/9 in round. Pile the filling into the centre. Roll out the remaining pastry large enough to cover the base. Brush the edges of the base with water and place the second round on top. Press together to seal and brush with egg. Bake for 45 minutes, or until golden.

Ratatouille & Fontina Strudel

This summer party pastry, made with mouth-watering layers of light filo, is filled with colourful Mediterranean vegetables.

Serves 6

INGREDIENTS
1 small aubergine, diced
45 ml/3 tbsp extra virgin
    olive oil
1 onion, sliced
2 garlic cloves, crushed
1 red pepper, seeded and sliced
1 yellow pepper, seeded
    and sliced
2 courgettes, cut into small chunks
pinch of dried mixed herbs
30 ml/2 tbsp pine nuts
30 ml/2 tbsp raisins
8 sheets filo pastry, thawed if frozen
50 g/2 oz/¼ cup butter, melted
130 g/4½ oz/generous 1 cup Fontina
    or Bel Paese cheese, cut into
    small cubes
salt and freshly ground
    black pepper
dressed mixed salad, to serve

1 Layer the diced aubergine in a colander, sprinkling each layer with salt. Drain over a sink for 20 minutes, then rinse and pat dry.

2 Heat the oil in a large frying pan and gently fry the onion, garlic, peppers and aubergine for about 10 minutes, stirring occasionally.

3 Add the courgettes, herbs and salt and pepper. Cook for 5 minutes, until softened. Cool to room temperature, then stir in the pine nuts and raisins.

4 Preheat the oven to 180°C/350°F/ Gas 4. Brush two sheets of filo pastry with melted butter. Lay the sheets side by side, overlapping by about 5 cm/ 2 in, to make a rectangle. Cover with the remaining filo, in the same way, brushing each layer with melted butter.

5 Spoon the vegetable mixture down one long side of the filo. Scatter the cheese over, then roll up to make a long sausage shape.

6 Transfer the roll to a non-stick baking sheet, curling it round in a circle. Brush with the remaining melted butter and bake for 30 minutes, until golden. Cool for 10 minutes, before slicing. Serve with mixed salad.

Spinach & Cheese Pie

The wonderful texture of filo pastry contrasts with the creamy richness of the spinach and ricotta filling in this flavoursome pie.

Serves 8

INGREDIENTS
1.5 kg/3–3½ lb fresh spinach,
    coarse stems removed
30 ml/2 tbsp olive oil
1 medium onion, finely chopped
30 ml/2 tbsp chopped fresh oregano or
    5 ml/1 tsp dried oregano
4 eggs
450 g/1 lb/2 cups Ricotta cheese
90 ml/6 tbsp freshly grated
    Parmesan cheese
grated nutmeg
60 ml/4 tbsp butter or
    margarine, melted
12 sheets filo pastry, thawed
    if frozen
salt and freshly ground
    black pepper
salad leaves, to serve

2 Heat the oil in a large pan. Add the onion and cook for about 5 minutes, until softened. Add the spinach and oregano and cook over a high heat, stirring frequently, for about 5 minutes, until most of the liquid has evaporated. Remove from the heat and let cool.

3 Beat the eggs in a large bowl. Stir in the Ricotta and Parmesan and season generously with nutmeg, salt and pepper. Stir in the spinach mixture.

4 Brush a 33 x 23 cm/13 x 9 in baking dish with some of the butter or margarine. Arrange half of the filo sheets in the base to cover evenly and extend about 2.5 cm/1 in up the sides. Brush with butter.

1 Preheat the oven to 190°C/375°F/ Gas 5. Stack handfuls of spinach leaves, roll them loosely, and cut into thin ribbons using a sharp knife.

5 Ladle in the spinach and cheese filling. Cover with the remaining filo pastry, tucking under the edge neatly. Brush with the remaining butter. Score the top with diamond shapes using a sharp knife.

6 Bake for about 30 minutes, until the pastry is golden brown. Cut into squares and serve hot, accompanied by mixed salad leaves.

COOK'S TIP: During preparation, always cover unused filo pastry with a damp dish towel or clear film to prevent it from drying out.

Cauliflower & Mushroom Gougère

Choux pastry, more often used for cream cakes, also makes a marvellous basis for savoury dishes.

Serves 4–6

INGREDIENTS
300 ml/½ pint/1¼ cups water
115 g/4 oz/½ cup butter or margarine,
    plus extra for greasing
150 g/5 oz/1¼ cups plain flour
4 eggs
115 g/4 oz/1 cup Gruyère or Cheddar
    cheese, finely diced
5 ml/1 tsp Dijon mustard
225 g/8 oz can tomatoes
15 ml/1 tbsp sunflower oil
15 g/½ oz/1 tbsp butter or margarine
1 onion, chopped
115 g/4 oz/1½ cups button mushrooms,
    halved if large
1 small cauliflower, broken into
    small florets
thyme sprig
salt and freshly ground
    black pepper

1 Preheat the oven to 200°C/400°F/ Gas 6 and grease a large ovenproof dish. Place the water and butter or margarine in a large saucepan and heat until the butter has melted. Remove from the heat and add all the flour at once. Beat well with a wooden spoon for about 30 seconds, until smooth. Allow to cool slightly.

2 Beat in the eggs, one at a time, and continue beating until the mixture is thick and glossy. Stir in the cheese and mustard and season with salt and pepper. Spread the mixture around the sides of the ovenproof dish, leaving a hollow in the centre for the filling.

3 To make the filling, process the tomatoes in a blender or food processor and then pour into a measuring jug. Add enough water to make up to 300 ml/½ pint/1¼ cups of liquid.

4 Heat the oil and butter or margarine in a saucepan and fry the chopped onion for about 3–4 minutes, until softened but not browned. Add the button mushrooms and cook for 2–3 minutes. Add the cauliflower florets and stir-fry for about 1 minute.

5 Add the tomato liquid, thyme and seasoning. Cook, uncovered, over a low heat for about 5 minutes, until the cauliflower is only just tender.

6 Spoon the mixture into the hollow in the ovenproof dish, adding all the liquid. Bake for about 35–40 minutes, until the pastry is well risen and golden brown.

49

Green Lentil Filo Pie

The delicate folds of light filo pastry conceal a tasty and substantial filling that would satisfy the hungriest appetite.

Serves 6

INGREDIENTS

175 g/6 oz/1 cup green lentils, soaked for
    30 minutes and drained
2 bay leaves
2 onions, sliced
1.2 litres/2 pints/5 cups
    vegetable stock
175 g/6 oz/¾ cup butter, melted
225 g/8 oz/generous 1 cup long grain rice
60 ml/4 tbsp chopped
    fresh parsley
30 ml/2 tbsp chopped fresh dill
1 egg, beaten
225 g/8 oz/3 cups mushrooms, sliced
about 8 sheets filo pastry, thawed
    if frozen
3 eggs, hard-boiled and sliced
salt and freshly ground
    black pepper

1 Cook the lentils with the bay leaves, 1 onion and half the stock for 25 minutes, until tender and thick. Season well, cool and set aside.

2 Gently fry the remaining onion in a pan with 30 ml/2 tbsp of the butter for 5 minutes. Stir in the rice then the remaining stock. Season, bring to the boil, then cover and cook gently for 15 minutes. Leave to stand, uncovered, for 5 minutes. Stir in the herbs, cool, then beat in the egg.

3 Fry the mushrooms in 45 ml/3 tbsp of the butter for 5 minutes, until they are just soft. Cool and set aside.

4 Brush the inside of a large, shallow ovenproof dish with more butter. Lay the sheets of filo in it, covering the base and making sure most of the pastry overhangs the sides. Brush each sheet with butter. Preheat the oven to 190°C/375°F/Gas 5.

5 Layer the rice, lentils and mushrooms in the dish, repeating the layers at least once and tucking the sliced hard-boiled eggs in between. Season as you layer and form an even mound of filling.

6 Bring up the sheets of filo over the filling, scrunching the top into attractive folds. Brush all over with the remaining butter and chill for 10 minutes. Bake for about 45 minutes, until golden and crisp. Allow to stand for 10 minutes before serving.

Apple Pie

A crisp piecrust tops a traditional American apple pie, which looks as pretty as a picture.

Serves 8

INGREDIENTS
225 g/8 oz/2 cups plain white flour
5 ml/1 tsp salt
115 g/4 oz/½ cup solid vegetable fat or lard
60–75 ml/4–5 tbsp water
15 ml/1 tbsp quick-cooking tapioca
900 g/2 lb tart eating apples, peeled
   and sliced
15 ml/1 tbsp fresh lemon juice
5 ml/1 tsp vanilla essence
90 g/3½ oz/½ cup sugar
2.5 ml/½ tsp ground cinnamon
15 g/½ oz/1 tbsp butter or margarine
1 egg yolk
10 ml/2 tsp whipping cream

1 Preheat the oven to 230°C/450°F/ Gas 8. For the pastry, sift the flour and salt into a mixing bowl. Using a pastry blender, cut in the fat or lard until the mixture resembles coarse crumbs. Sprinkle in the water, 15 ml/1 tbsp at a time, tossing lightly with your fingertips or with a fork until the dough forms a ball.

2 Divide the dough in half and shape each half into a ball. On a lightly floured surface, roll out one of the balls to a round about 30 cm/12 in in diameter.

3 Use it to line a 23 cm/9 in pie dish. Trim off the excess dough. Sprinkle the tapioca over the base of the pastry case.

4 Roll out the remaining dough. With a sharp knife, cut out eight large leaf shapes. Cut the trimmings into small leaf shapes. Score the leaves with the back of the knife to mark veins.

5 In a bowl, toss the apples with the lemon juice, vanilla, sugar and cinnamon. Fill the pastry case with the apple mixture and dot with the butter or margarine.

6 Arrange the large pastry leaves in a decorative pattern on top. Decorate the edge with small leaves. Mix together the egg yolk and cream and brush over the leaves to glaze. Bake for 10 minutes, then reduce the temperature to 180°C/350°F/ Gas 4 and continue baking for 35–45 minutes. Cool on a wire rack.

Pear Tarte Tatin with Cardamom

Crispy puff pastry snugly encloses tasty caramelized pears in this spicy upside-down tart.

Serves 4

INGREDIENTS
50 g/2 oz/¼ cup butter, softened
50 g/2 oz/¼ cup caster sugar
seeds from 10 cardamoms
225 g/8 oz puff pastry, thawed if frozen
3 ripe pears, peeled, cored and
    halved lengthways
cream, to serve

1 Preheat the oven to 220°C/425°F/Gas 7. Spread the butter over the base of an 18 cm/7 in heavy-based cake tin or an ovenproof omelette pan. Spread the sugar evenly over the base of the tin or pan. Scatter the cardamom seeds over the sugar.

2 On a floured surface, roll out the puff pastry to a round slightly larger than the tin or pan. Prick the pastry lightly, then transfer it to a baking sheet and chill while you prepare the filling.

3 Arrange the pears, rounded side down, on the butter and sugar. Set the cake tin or omelette pan over a medium heat until the sugar melts and begins to bubble. If any areas are browning more than others, move the pan, but do not stir.

4 As soon as the sugar has caramelized, remove the tin or pan carefully from the heat. Place the pastry on top, tucking the edges down the side of the pan. Transfer to the oven and bake for 25 minutes, until well risen and golden.

5 Leave the tart in the tin or pan for 2–3 minutes until the juices have stopped bubbling. Invert the tin over a plate and shake to release the tart. It may be necessary to slide a spatula underneath the pears to loosen them. Serve the tart warm with cream.

Lemon Tart

This is one of the classic French desserts, and it is difficult to beat: a rich lemon curd, encased in crisp pastry.

Serves 6

INGREDIENTS
225 g/8 oz/2 cups plain flour
115 g/4 oz/½ cup butter, diced
30 ml/2 tbsp icing sugar
1 egg, beaten, for the pastry
5 ml/1 tsp vanilla essence
6 eggs, beaten, for the filling
350 g/12 oz/1¾ cups caster sugar
115 g/4 oz/½ cup unsalted butter
grated rind and juice of 4 lemons
icing sugar, for dusting

1 Preheat the oven to 200°C/400°F/ Gas 6. Sift the flour into a bowl, add the diced butter, and work with your fingertips until the mixture resembles fine breadcrumbs. Stir in the icing sugar.

2 Add the egg, vanilla essence and a scant tablespoon of cold water, then work to a dough.

3 Roll out the pastry on a floured surface and use to line a 23 cm/9 in tart tin. Line with foil or greaseproof paper and fill with baking beans. Bake for 10 minutes.

4 For the filling, put the eggs, sugar and butter into a pan and stir over a low heat until the sugar has dissolved. Add the lemon rind and juice, and continue cooking, stirring, until the lemon curd has thickened slightly.

5 Pour the mixture into the pastry case. Bake for 20 minutes, until just set. Transfer to a wire rack to cool. Dust with icing sugar before serving.

Blueberry Pie

You will simply love this easy-to-make double-crust pie, simply crammed full of juicy summer fruit.

Serves 6–8

INGREDIENTS
350 g/12 oz/3 cups plain white flour
2.5 ml/½ tsp salt
175 g/6 oz/⅔ cup fat, chilled and diced
60–75 ml/4–5 tbsp iced water
500 g/1¼ lb blueberries
165 g/5½ oz/¾ cup caster sugar
45 ml/3 tbsp plain flour
5 ml/1 tsp grated orange rind
1.5 ml/¼ tsp grated nutmeg
30 ml/2 tbsp orange juice
5 ml/1 tsp lemon juice

1 Make the shortcrust pastry following the instructions from the techniques section. Preheat the oven to 190°C/375°F/Gas 5. Roll out half the pastry and use to line a 23 cm/9 in pie tin that is about 5 cm/2 in deep.

2 Combine the blueberries, 150 g/ 5 oz/scant ¾ cup of the sugar, the flour, orange rind and nutmeg in a bowl. Toss gently to coat the fruit.

3 Pour the blueberry mixture on to the pastry case. Sprinkle over the citrus juices. Moisten the pie edge with water.

4 Roll out the remaining pastry and cut out decorative holes using a small biscuit cutter. Cover the pie.

5 Cut out a few more shapes from the trimmings. Press the edges to seal and finish as desired. Decorate the top with the shaped pastry trimmings. Brush lightly with water and sprinkle with the remaining caster sugar.

6 Bake the pie for about 45 minutes, until golden brown and crisp. Serve warm or at room temperature.

VARIATION: This pie would also work well with blackberries.

Pecan Pie

Melt-in-the-mouth pastry encloses the sweet, rich filling of this popular American pie. A delicious dessert served with cream or ice cream.

Serves 6

INGREDIENTS
200 g/7 oz/1¾ cups plain flour
pinch of salt
115 g/4 oz/½ cup butter
30–60 ml/2–4 tbsp iced water
3 eggs
pinch of salt
5 ml/1 tsp vanilla essence
200 g/7 oz/¾ cup dark
   brown sugar
60 ml/4 tbsp golden syrup
50 g/2 oz/4 tbsp butter, melted
115 g/4 oz/1 cup chopped pecan kernels,
   plus 12 pecan halves
whipped cream or vanilla ice cream,
   to serve

1 Mix the flour with a pinch of salt, then rub in the butter with the fingertips until the mixture resembles fine breadcrumbs. Add iced water a little at a time, mixing first with a fork. Gather into a dough.

2 Wrap the dough in clear film and chill for 30 minutes. Preheat the oven to 190°C/375°F/Gas 5.

3 Grease a 20 cm/8 in loose-based flan tin. Roll out the pastry and use to line the tin.

4 Run the rolling pin over the top of the tin to sever the surplus pastry.

5 Prick the pastry base and line with foil and baking beans. Bake blind for 15 minutes, then remove the foil and bake for a further 5 minutes. Take the pastry case from the oven and lower the temperature to 180°C/350°F/Gas 4.

6 Meanwhile, to make the filling, beat the eggs lightly with the salt and vanilla essence, then beat in the sugar, syrup and melted butter. Mix in the chopped pecans.

7 Spread the mixture in the pastry case and bake for 15 minutes. Remove from the oven and stud with the pecan halves in a circle.

8 Return to the oven and bake for a further 20–25 minutes until cooked through. Cool the pie for 10–15 minutes and serve warm with whipped cream or a scoop of vanilla ice cream.

Chocolate Profiteroles

These choux pastry puffs are extremely easy to make, but look very impressive. This unusual version includes a rich chocolate glaze.

Makes 12 large or 24 small profiteroles

INGREDIENTS
150 g/5 oz/¾ cup plain flour
25 g/1 oz/¼ cup unsweetened cocoa
250 ml/8 fl oz/1 cup water
2.5 ml/½ tsp salt
15 ml/1 tbsp sugar
115 g/4 oz/½ cup unsalted butter, cut
    into pieces
4–5 eggs
600 ml/1 pint/2½ cups whipping cream
15 ml/1 tbsp each cocoa and hot water,
    blended together and cooled
50 g/2 oz/4 tbsp unsalted butter, cut
    into pieces
225 g/8 oz plain chocolate, chopped
15 ml/1 tbsp golden syrup
5 ml/1 tsp vanilla essence

1 Preheat the oven to 220°C/425°F/ Gas 7. Lightly grease 1 or 2 large baking sheets. Sift together the flour and cocoa into a bowl. Bring the water, salt, sugar and butter to the boil in a saucepan.

2 Remove from the heat and add the flour mixture all at once, stirring vigorously until the mixture pulls away from the side of the pan. Return the pan to the heat for 1 minute, beating constantly. Remove from the heat.

3 Beat in four of the eggs, one at a time. If the mixture is too dry, beat the fifth egg lightly and add to the dough a little at a time until you reach a dropping consistency. Spoon the mixture into a large icing bag fitted with a large star nozzle. Pipe 12 or 24 mounds 5 cm/2 in apart on the baking sheet.

4 Bake for 35–40 minutes, until puffed and firm. Using a serrated knife, slice off the top third of each cake. Place cut-side up on the baking sheet and return to the switched-off oven for 5–10 minutes to dry out. Remove to a wire rack to cool.

5 Whip 300 ml/½ pint/1¼ cups cream and add the cocoa mixture. Using a piping bag, fill each puff base with cream, then cover each with its top. Arrange on a serving plate.

6 In a medium saucepan over a low heat, heat the remaining cream, butter, chocolate, syrup and vanilla until smooth, stirring frequently. Remove from heat and cool for 20–30 minutes, until slightly thickened. Pour a little sauce over each of the profiteroles and serve warm or cold.

Index

This edition published by Hermes House

Hermes House is an imprint of
Anness Publishing Limited
Hermes House, 88–89 Blackfriars Road, London SE1 8HA

Publisher: Joanna Lorenz
Editor: Valerie Ferguson
Series Designer: Bobbie Colgate Stone
Designer: Andrew Heath
Production Controller: Joanna King

Recipes contributed by: Alex Barker, Frances Cleary, Roz
Denny, Matthew Drennan, Joanna Farrow,
Shirley Gill, Rebekah Hassan, Christine Ingram,
Ruby Le Bois, Lesley Mackley, Norma Macmillan,
Sue Maggs, Norma Miller, Sallie Morris, Annie Nichols,
Katherine Richmond, Anne Sheasby, Jenny Stacey,
Liz Trigg, Steven Wheeler

Photography: William Adams-Lingwood, Karl Adamson,
Steve Baxter, James Duncan, John Freeman,
Michelle Garrett, John Heseltine, Amanda Heywood,
David Jordan, Patrick McLeavey, Michael Michaels,
Thomas Odulate

Notes:
For all recipes, quantities are given in both metric and
imperial measures and, where appropriate, measures are
also given in standard cups and spoons.
Follow one set, but not a mixture, because they are
not interchangeable.

Standard spoon and cup measures are level.

1 tsp = 5 ml   1 tbsp =15 ml

1 cup = 250 ml/8 fl oz

Australian standard tablespoons are 20 ml.
Australian readers should use 3 tsp in place of 1 tbsp for
measuring small quantities of gelatine, cornflour, salt, etc.

Medium eggs are used unless otherwise stated.

Printed and bound in China